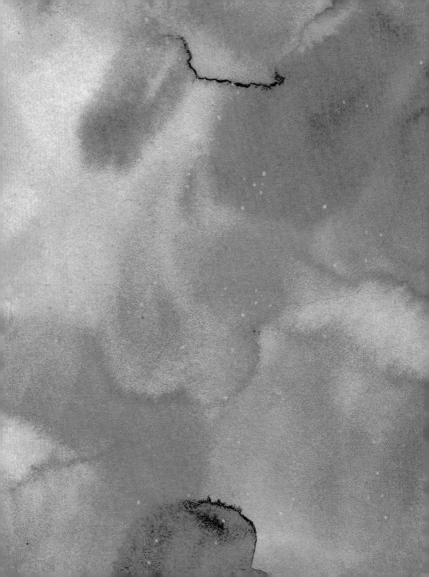

AN INTRODUCTION TO MAGIC

AN INTRODUCTION TO MAGIC

A Guide to Crystals, Fairies, Palmistry, Tarot, and the Zodiac

Nikki Van De Car, Mikaila Adriance,
Pliny T. Young, Eugene Fletcher

RUNNING PRESS
PHILADELPHIA

From *Crystals 500-Piece Puzzle* published by RP Studio in 2022; *Fairies 2-in-1 Double-Sided 500-Piece Puzzle*, published by RP Studio in 2023; *Palmistry 500-Piece Puzzle*, published by RP Studio in 2022; *Tarot 500-Piece Puzzle*, published by RP Studio in 2021; *Zodiac 500-Piece Puzzle*, published by RP Studio in 2021.

Running Press
Hachette Book Group
1290 Avenue of the Americas, New York, NY 10104
www.runningpress.com
@Running_Press

Published by Running Press, an imprint of Hachette Book Group, Inc. The Running Press name and logo are trademarks of Hachette Book Group, Inc.

Print book cover design by Justine Kelley. Interior design by Justine Kelley based on original designs by Jenna McBride (Crystals, Palmistry, and Tarot chapters), Tanvi Baghele (Fairies chapter), and Susan Van Horn (Zodiac chapter).

Text credits: Crystals chapter by Pliny T. Young; Fairies chapter by Eugene Fletcher; Palmistry chapter by Mikaila Adriance; Tarot and Zodiac chapters by Nikki Van De Car

Library of Congress Cataloging-in-Publication Data has been applied for.

ISBNs: 978-0-7624-8769-1 (hardcover), 978-0-7624-8770-7 (ebook)

Printed in China

1010

10 9 8 7 6 5 4 3 2 1

CONTENTS

AN INTRODUCTION

Magic is a luminous thread that is woven through the tapestry of humankind. From influencing the decisions we make, to shedding light on truths within ourselves and others, and even offering a glimpse of future possibilities, there is no corner of our lives in which magic is *not* present. It silently exists in the quiet moments of coincidence that occur in your daily life, just as it does in the more significant, serendipitous events that occasionally happen. You just need to learn where, when, and how to look for it. This primer will properly set you up to do just that.

Curiosity has long brought people to the threshold of the magical realm, searching for knowledge, truth, and light. These inquisitive people are sometimes referred to as

Seekers. If you, too, are a Seeker and desire to begin your own exploration of the esoteric, we welcome you. It is only natural, after all, to speculate about the things that lie just beyond our physical world.

Within these enlightening and richly illustrated pages, you will unearth information on some of the most important and fundamental magical topics: Crystals, Fairies, Palmistry, Tarot, and the Zodiac. These topics aren't chosen randomly, of course. They each hold the ingredients necessary for an informed exploration of magic, one that is positive, fun, thoughtful, and inspiring. Plus, many other areas of magic are built upon these specific topics and practices; you may even find yourself referencing this information again should you choose to further your magical studies.

The first topic we will uncover in this primer is Crystal magic. Scientifically speaking, crystals are a consolidation of elements that have been compressed within the earth over millions of years to form the glistening gemstones we often find in jewelry and other accessories. You might already be familiar with some, like the popular rose quartz and amethyst. Undoubtedly alluring, a crystal's physical appearance plays a large role in its magic. The candy-pink rose quartz has a completely different purpose than the moody purple amethyst does, just as a smooth, tumbled gemstone is used in different ways than a carved crystal wand is. For reasons beyond their physical attributes, crystals have been regarded throughout history as essential for any type of magic since they are believed to hold ancient energy, wisdom, and powers. Sprouting from these beliefs, and in conjunction with the discipline of meditation and the study of the chakras, the practice of crystal healing and meditation was created. Whether you are looking to clear your heart chakra of negative energy or simply want to meditate to obtain some creative inspiration, there's a crystal that can help do the job.

Prepare to learn about some of the most common crystals and their uses, and maybe even reveal the secrets hidden behind their shimmering facets.

Following Crystals, we will turn our attention to Fairies. Fairies are far more fascinating than how they are often portrayed in media. They have a rich and expansive history that runs deeply through the archives of humanity—the belief of their existence can be found in countries and cultures the world over, with each interpretation more unique than the next. You will learn about Fairies found in lands both near and far, and ones that have emerged from bygone eras like the Medieval ages, soaring all the way to Fae found in modern times. As you will come to see, the magic of these ethereal beings is held in the lure of their presence and the feelings of wonder they inspire within everyone. Fairies offer humans a special connection to nature that isn't easily found. These mystical creatures will remind you to not only respect the earth, but to also protect it so that we can revel in its beauty for generations to come.

Next, we will venture into the ancient study of Palmistry. Did you know that the shape of your palm may reveal certain aspects of your personality, like whether you have a tendency for empathy or not? Or that there is a particular line on your palm, known as the Life Line, that can suggest if you will have a fruitful and happy life? Palmistry, commonly known as palm reading, goes far beyond and is even more compelling than the stereotypes that often come with the name. In this section, we will dive into the history and practice of palm reading while unveiling the tangible secrets your hands hold. Who would have thought that magic was as close as your fingertips?

Tarot, with its symbolism and prophetic guidance, is the next area of focus. This section will review the card basics: the Major Arcana, the Minor Arcana, the suits, and some of the most popular card spreads used. While they are well-known for the iconic images they display, it is the cards' metaphysical abilities that have been revered for ages. You will learn that the Tarot deck isn't a fortune-telling instrument; rather, the cards are a vessel used to foster connection to your intuition, to help you find the courage to pursue your dreams, and to assist you when faced with making tough decisions. You will also learn how to interpret the cards when they are pulled as well as the obscure meanings each card possesses. The Tarot deck holds endless potential, and learning how to properly use it can open doors you never even knew existed.

The last (and perhaps most widely known) magical subject in this compendium is the Zodiac. For eons, humans have gazed upon the night sky and its celestial bodies all while searching for insight into various aspects of their lives. In this section, you will learn about the twelve signs of Western astrology; the constellations, symbols, and characteristics associated with each of these signs; and more. The divine secrets and truths the twinkling constellations and spinning planets hold are older than life itself—it is no wonder the study of the Zodiac has inspired awe equally as long.

It's clear why these topics and practices have endured millennia—they offer Seekers like you comfort during times of uncertainty; inspiration for living a life of fulfillment and joy; optimism for what the future holds. Let this primer be a lighted torch with which you confidently enter the realm of magic and mysticism, ready to forge your unique path on the way to self-discovery. When you are ready, these practices are just as eager to be discovered as you are to discover them. But do remember: The subjects in this book are not rules you *need* to live by, nor are they the only way to discover both universal and self-truths. They are simply tools to use and suggestions to apply when you feel a situation calls for them.

Now, Seeker, go forth and explore all there is to discover; there is much to learn and reveal.

CHAPTER 1

Crystals

AUTHOR'S NOTE

My understandings of crystals, gems, and precious stones came primarily by way of friends, acquaintances, and my own meditation and holistic-living practices.

The information in this book is not a replacement for professional medical advice. If you're sick, please consult with your doctor.

The following merely offers a lantern through the darkness, or at least a frame of reference for the next time someone places a crystal to your brow . . .

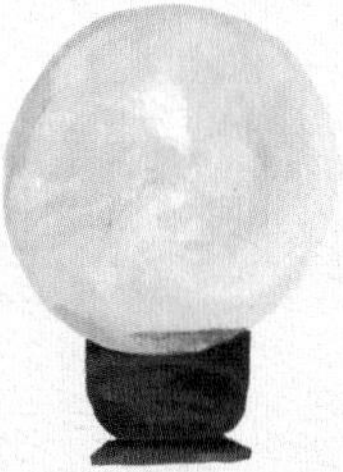

A (BRIEF) HISTORY OF CRYSTALS

Crystals, precious stones, gems, and minerals spring naturally from the earth. Compacted over millions of years, they are comprised of elements that have been trapped in various geologic conditions.

Our obsession with these boiled, compressed, and excoriated element conglomerations dates back to the ancients, who credited crystals with healing powers and abilities. Even today, crystals are used in the making of computers, surgical tools, automobile engines, and spaceships. From jewelry to architecture, the arts to the sciences, crystals have been fundamental in the construction of our spaces (and, if your watch happens to be quartz-powered, in the construction of time as well).

Yet, the true power of "crystal magic" lies primarily in the energy inherent in how we appreciate crystals, gems, and stones. Much has been written about the ancient art of laying stones on the body for protection, teaching, and healing (known as "grid work" or "reiki"). A lot has been

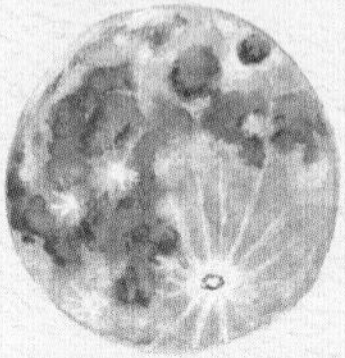

written as well about the role that crystals play in radiating one's intentions out into the cosmos. The origins of these practices lie in humankind's enduring regard for these geologic miracles.

By simply paying attention to beauty and form, one's mind finds ways to push out those everyday distractions that remove us from the present—namely fear, pain, hunger, and death.

If you are reading this, then you are capable of setting an intention with your energy.

Only one question remains: W*hat is your intention*?

THE INFLUENCE OF COLOR

Throughout the history of our known world, interpretations of color have been based mostly on correspondences recorded between community leaders. Understanding these reference points can help guide and inspire you as you address different goals and intentions.

Here is a list of the primary colors along with some of their observed associations:

BLACK, taking in all wavelengths, detoxifies and protects the body from harm.

BROWN, like black, detoxifies and grounds one's energy, increasing connection with the earth.

RED energizes the body and the brain. The color of blood and passion, it resonates with one's sex drive and reproductive systems.

PINK heals emotional imbalance and gently energizes the nervous system.

◇◇◇

ORANGE energizes you mentally and creatively. It stimulates personal power.

◇◇◇

YELLOW stimulates the nervous system, resonating mental energy via neurotransmitters, the adrenal glands, and the intestines. As the color of the sun, yellow has always had a powerful influence on the way humankind experiences reality.

◇◇◇

GREEN is calming. As the color of new life, it speaks to our hearts and our eyes.

◇◇◇

BLUE is the color of healing by way of thought. Just the sight of blue is reported, in many cases, to reduce blood pressure.

◇◇◇

INDIGO is a mystical color, one of power and contemplation. Among many other disciplines, it is used in chromotherapy to treat alcoholism and masochism.

VIOLET AND PURPLE are often the colors of royalty, resonating in the pituitary gland and said to regulate the metabolism and regenerate the body.

WHITE has long been recognized as a color of purity and wisdom. As the color of light and illumination, it is composed of all colors in equilibrium, homeostasis, and balance.

A given stone may contain one or all these colors. When combined, the synergies between the hues can lead to a variety of interpretations.

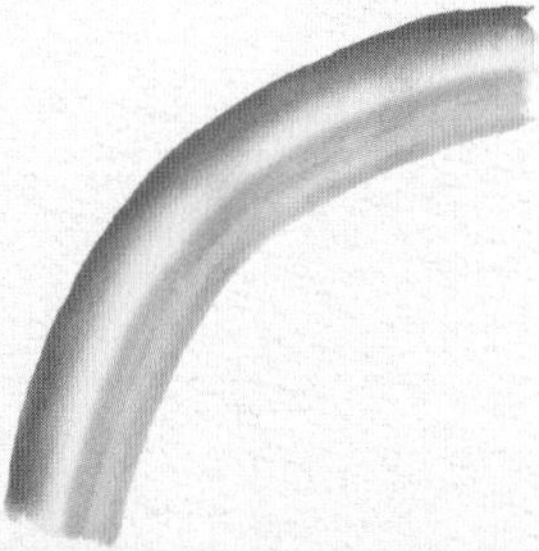

SHAPE & SIZE

Crystals, gems, and healing stones come in manifold shapes and sizes, which can assist in "dialing in" one's intentions. After mining, many crystals are artificially shaped by lapidary artists, enhancing their beauty and influence.

Like color, geometric shape, dimension, and magnitude can all greatly impact the effect of a crystal on its user. By examining the finer details, you can use a stone's geometry to reveal and manipulate energetic intention.

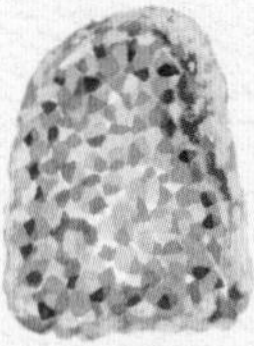

GEODE: A small cavity inside a larger rock lined with crystals and other minerals, it has an almost "cave-like" structure, cultivating protection, radiance, and spiritual growth.

DOUBLE-TERMINATED: A crystal with two terminating points on opposing ends, allowing its user to both draw energy in and emanate energy out.

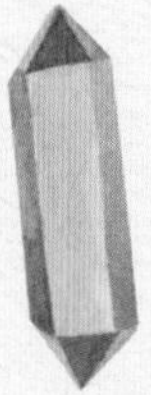

WAND: A long, cylindrical crystal, usually without termination, which crystal workers use to externally "push" energy around and within the body.

SCEPTER: A central point crystal with another, stouter crystal wrapped around its base, which is said to create a greater reservoir for energetic cultivation.

PHANTOM: A crystal, often pyramidal in shape, laid down in layers within another type of crystal, resembling hierarchical structures.

POINT: Longer, six-faced crystals joined to form a point (also called a "termination"). Placing the point toward the body is said to channel intention inward, while pointing away beams those same aspirations outward, driving away negativity.

CLUSTER: Several point crystals with a common base, often varied in size, which radiates out energy in different directions.

BED: Many smaller crystals spread over a matrix groundmass base, radiating low but consistent energy within the surrounding atmosphere.

BALL: Artificially shaped from a larger piece of crystal, a ball emits power in all directions equally.

PALM: Flat or rounded stones said to soothe the mind and help focus one's intention.

MANIFESTATION: A crystal with a smaller crystal encased within that assists in cultivating new intention or revealing trapped energy in need of release.

APPRECIATING YOUR STONE

In addition to color, shape, and size, there are a handful of further considerations that can greatly enhance your appreciation of a given stone.

The Source of Your Stone

Things, good or bad, come to us by one of two routes: Some we find, some we are gifted. Upon encountering such things, we have the choice to protect or discard. Crystals, as it turns out, are no different.

As with any gift, its giver can be a source of rejuvenating appreciation and affirmation for the person receiving the gift. Bonds of friendship, collaboration, and even love can help contextualize the crystal, as its powers of inherent beauty, intention storage, and spiritual healing are reinforced by whoever helped manifest those elements by gifting this crystal to you in the first place. Alternatively, happening upon a particular crystal in a store or amid the natural world (if you're really lucky) can be a practically mystical experience. Out of all the people in the world, this crystal found you. What are the chances?

Whether you come upon a crystal in your travels, by gift, or by chance, it is now your charge. You decide whether to keep it warm or cold, displayed or secret. It is said that the healing properties in stones are revitalized by the sun. Honoring our things with a role and responsibility in our lives helps us appreciate them, and crystals are no different.

The Appearance of Your Stone

Each crystal, upon close examination, contains its own energetic signature. Some people refer to this as a stone's "personality" while others credit crystals with the possession of magical abilities.

From a more grounded perspective, simply consider the uniqueness of your stone. There isn't another exactly like it in the world.

Whenever you come across a crystal, take a moment to examine it with as many senses as you can. Take time to appreciate its constituted form.

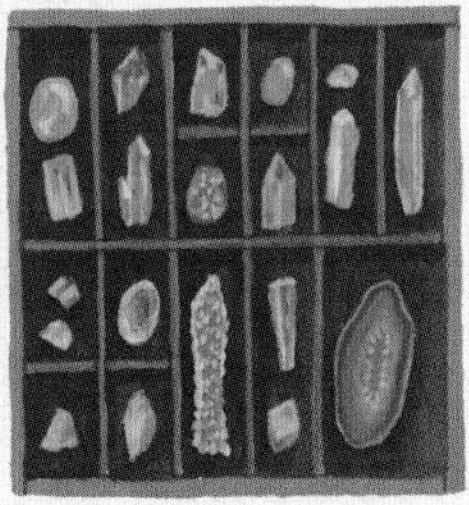

The Meaning of Your Stone

When examining a stone, we have the opportunity to appreciate something greater. By paying attention to the tracks of color, dimensions of shapes, and lines of inquiry, one can find all sorts of meanings and permutations within. All one must do is look.

MEDITATION WITH CRYSTALS

If you haven't yet introduced meditation into your daily life, then you and a trusted crystal may consider embarking on the journey together.

In this case, you may think of the stone as a symbolic concentration object, a place to focus your energy. Any healing crystal can be used as a meditation partner, and the more you educate yourself about stones, their legacy, and their perceived properties, the better you will be at choosing the right crystal for your intention.

Before meditating with a crystal, take a moment to consider it—hold it gently and get a sense for the energetic vibrations you receive. If you and the stone are in accord, you should feel a sense of calm, expansion, and peace. (This process is known in the crystal community as "attunement.")

If this is your first time meditating with a crystal, it is advised that you soak it in a warm saltwater bath

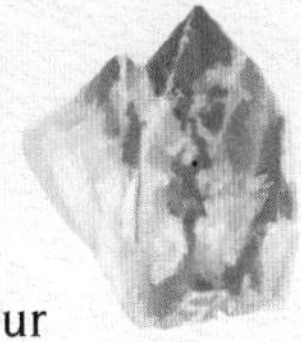

to cleanse it (both literally and within your mind's eye) of any previous and unintended energies. With this practice, you can meditate comfortably in the knowledge that your meditation partner is free of past energies and empowered for the journey ahead.

The Effects of Meditation on the Human Body

Meditation works on a human's physical and ethereal self via a powerful combination of breath, posture, mantras, and mental focus.

Contemporary medicine ascribes responsibility to the nerve plexuses and endocrine glands for the movement of healthy vitality throughout the body. Ancient tradition refers to these same structures by the more spiritual term "chakras," which are detailed in the following diagram.

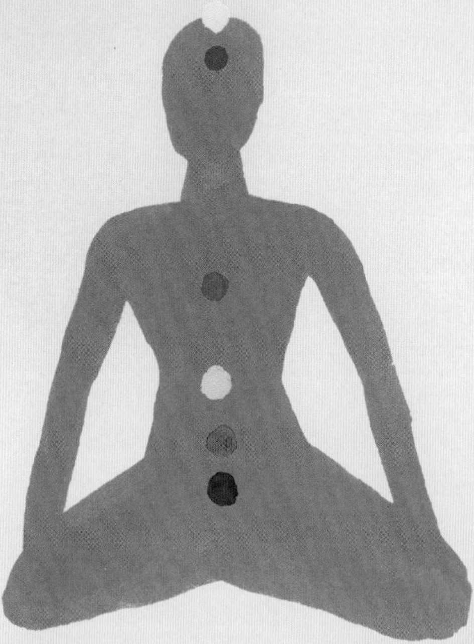

CROWN CHAKRA (Top of Head / Pineal Gland)

Sanskrit Name: Sahasrara | **Colors:** White, Clear

Associated Crystals: Selenite, Clear Quartz, Diamond, Heliodor

THIRD EYE CHAKRA (Brain / Pituitary Gland)

Sanskrit Name: Ajna | **Colors:** Indigo, Purple

Associated Crystals: Sodalite, Lapis, Azurite, Sugilite, Fluorite, Amethyst, Sapphire

THROAT CHAKRA (Pharyngeal Plexus / Thyroid)

Sanskrit Name: Visuddhu | **Color:** Blue

Associated Crystals: Amazonite, Turquoise, Chrysocolla, Celestite, Aquamarine, Gem Silica, Blue Lace Agate

HEART CHAKRA (Cardiac Plexus / Thymus)

Sanskrit Name: Anahata | **Colors:** Green, Pink

Associated Crystals: Rhodochrosite, Moonstone, Opal, Rose Quartz, Kunzite, Pink Tourmaline, Green Tourmaline, Adventurine, Emerald, Dioptase, Morganite

SOLAR PLEXUS CHAKRA (Navel / Adrenal Gland)

Sanskrit Name: Manipura | **Colors:** Orange, Yellow, Yellow Green

Associated Crystals: Sulphur, Citrine, Topaz, Apatite, Calcite, Malachite, Peridot, Green Tourmaline

SACRAL CHAKRA (Lower Abdomen / Leydig Cells)

Sanskrit Name: Svadhisthana | **Colors:** Red, Orange

Associated Crystals: Garnet, Ruby, Carnelian, Wulfenite, Citrine, Amber

ROOT CHAKRA (Base of Spine / Gonads)

Sanskrit Name: Muladhara | **Colors:** Black, Deep Red

Associated Crystals: Obsidian, Smoky Quartz, Bloodstone, Onyx, Rhodonite, Garnet

There are seven chakras widely considered to be present in the human body, though different disciplines and belief structures identify others. For example, an eighth, more ethereal chakra refers to one's aura, or bioelectric field, located outside the body. This chakra is colloquially referred to as one's "energy" or "vibe" and is known among crystal healers as the "Soul Star Chakra."

Energy works up through the chakras, one to eight, culminating in the practice and presentation of an individual's personhood.

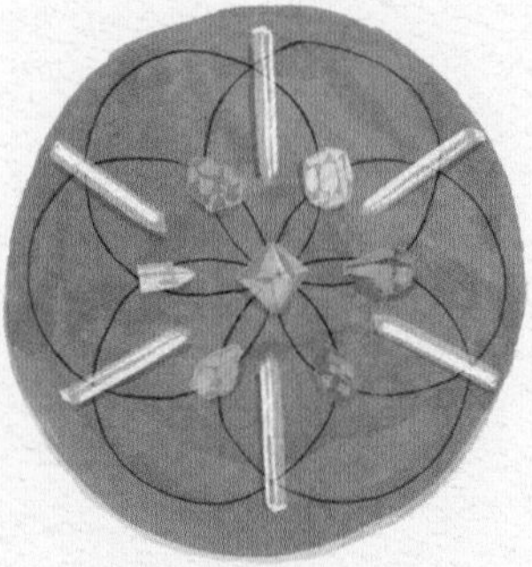

How to Meditate with Your Crystal

Below is a quick, easy, and totally free way to begin meditating right now. You need only to find a safe, quiet, and private space for approximately 10–15 minutes.

During your meditation, hold, wear, or place the crystal within your visual or conscious field, to be used as an object of mental focus.

1 | Sit either cross-legged or upright in a chair, with your head held high and your core muscles flexed to straighten your spine.

2 | Take 3 deep breaths—inhaling through the nose and exhaling through the mouth.

3 | Once completed, breathe normally, counting your breaths from 1 to 10. Once you have reached 10, speak your mantra (see page 23) to yourself as you exhale, then go back to 1.

4 | Once you feel relaxed, calm, or rejuvenated (estimated time: 10–15 minutes), take 3 more deep breaths, making the final exhalation as long as you are physically able.

5 | Repeat your mantra to yourself one last time.

Practice this meditation any time you are stressed and, if possible, daily when you wake up and before you go to sleep.

Finding a Mantra

Cultivating a mantra of your own is as simple as writing down or speaking aloud a phrase that is particularly inspirational to you based on your intention.

Sound is, at its core, vibration. These vibrations have been detected in practically every corner of the known universe, and the psychoactive potential of specific sounds has been recognized for thousands of years. In turn, the chanting of mantras—specific phrases of resonance—has been an integral component of spiritual practice in every culture, in every period of time, the world over.

To get you started, here are a few powerful and timeless mantras for your consideration:

"Om"

ORIGIN: Antiquity

MEANING: Composed of the three sounds *ah*, *oh*, and *m*, this mantra is widely recognized as the most fundamental sound in the universe, referring to the force of creation.

"Sat Nam"

ORIGINS: Kundalini Yoga

MEANING: Truth is my identity.

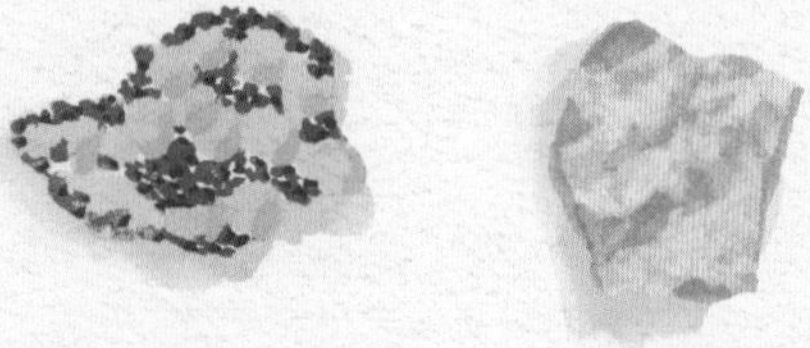

"Healthy Am I, Happy Am I, Holy Am I"

ORIGIN: Modern Nonsectarian

MEANING: Health, happiness, and holiness are one in the eyes of God.

You may "program" the crystal with your mantra by simply speaking it into the crystal before meditating, which will mentally affirm the new, more positive reality you are attempting to cultivate. After meditation, this programmed crystal can be carried with you, held, looked at, or thought upon during your day. It is a physical token that can help you retain your mantra even in the darkest times, emanating back to you the vision you wish to manifest.

Realigning the Brain

It is said that how we think has an incredible impact on the way we live.

The roots of this have been identified physically within our biology via the brain's hypothalamus. Nearly all human experience exists within a spectrum of satisfaction and withdrawal from external resources, and our most celebrated and debilitating emotional experiences are correlated with the release of neuropeptides. When encountering external stimuli, like food or temperature, the hypothalamus releases neuropeptides in order to bring the body

back to homeostasis, which is largely controlled by the predeterminations of our sense memory.

As such, even a simple conscious meditation practice can begin to alleviate stresses and/or realign chakra energy, improve plexus performance, and stimulate endocrine function. This allows us to tackle our preconceived notions of dependency and expand our consciousness to new levels.

In this way, you can shape your own reality, including your space, your time, and your future.

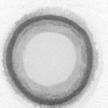

EPILOGUE

Your relationship with any given stone is yours alone.

As with any of the resources that our world provides, abuse, misuse, and malcontent can turn crystals' powers against us.

So, respect your crystals. Work with them the way you would with a loved one. Treat them as you would like to be treated, and you can expect to enjoy many years of life-affirming companionship.

Appreciate the reality that we share with other people, our homes, and the very earth itself.

We are, all of us, made from atoms, the elegant dance of neutrons, protons, and electrons. And a dance can only be experienced when we are free from distraction.

CHAPTER 2
Fairies

IT'S LIKELY YOU ALREADY KNOW a thing or two about fairies and have perhaps even encountered a few in your lifetime or have felt their magical presence. Fairies, one of the most beloved creatures of Fae, are typically small, though they should not be underestimated for their size. Throughout history, they've been known to be fierce, temperamental, and capricious, with a penchant for playing tricks, and their attitude can change from friendly to ferocious without warning if they are offended.

The fairies featured in this chapter reflect a wide range of cultures and histories. From Korea to Ireland, from Senegal to the Louisiana Bayou, all around the world, people have believed in the concept of a small enchanted being who has the power to affect change. But how a fairy favors you ultimately depends on the kind of energy you exude. They tend to like those who seek them out, who believe in their ability to bestow luck and take it away. Get to know these cunning shape-shifters, and they just might bring new joy and laughter into your life, even stirring up a little trouble every now and then, hopefully only when it's necessary.

JOAN THE WAD

JOAN THE WAD, A FAIRY OF CORNISH FOLKLORE, IS often depicted naked on metal charms that were traditionally worn or carried for good luck. The word *wad* is an ancient Cornish term meaning "torch." Known as a benevolent queen of the pixies, Joan the Wad bestows light upon those who travel in the depths of the night, especially those who seek her.

SPRITES

SPRITES ARE A COMMON TYPE OF FAIRY WITH insect-like wings, who glow like fireflies in the dark. It's possible you have seen one before in the woods or even just your backyard and mistaken them for an insect or flower. They are playful by nature and live in harmony with birds, beetles, butterflies—everything in their natural surroundings, including each other.

THE DOKKAEBI

IN KOREAN FOLKLORE, THE DOKKAEBI ARE CREATURES who closely resemble goblins. Like other fairies, they are nature deities who possess powers to either help humans or play tricks on them, bestowing good fortune or bad, depending on the situation. Often wearing the traditional Korean hanbok, they are known to possess inanimate objects.

ELEMENTAL FAIRIES

ELEMENTAL FAIRIES ARE ASSOCIATED WITH THE four classic elements: air, fire, water, and earth. When these elements are in balance, the physical world is healthy; as a result, the spiritual world is, too. Elemental fairies are everywhere, guarding everything from our beaches and mountains to our backyards and gardens. If you've ever felt peaceful sitting by the water or under a tree, it's likely that elemental fairies were nearby, working their magic.

MAMI WATA

MAMI WATA (PIDGIN ENGLISH FOR "MOTHER WATER") is a water spirit of African folklore who is known for being beautiful, seductive, and nurturing, as well as dangerous and destructive. A powerful being who contains multitudes and who has the ability to bestow good or bad fortune usually in the form of money, she has been celebrated throughout Africa by works of art that pay tribute to her sacred connection with water. Half woman and half fish, Mami Wata resembles a mermaid and appears as a snake charmer in many interpretations, though her image is one that has changed repeatedly over the years, taking on aspects of different cultures. Her form is fluid, just like the water with which she has such affinity.

MORGANA LE FAY

MORGANA LE FAY IS A MYSTERIOUS FAIRY OF ARTHURIAN legend, whose only consistent trait is perhaps that she is by nature inconsistent, a shape-shifter who takes on many forms. In some stories, she can fly and literally morph into different shapes. In others, she's an instigator who stirs up trouble in King Arthur's court, some even saying she seduced the magician Merlin in order to obtain his knowledge of spells. In other accounts still, she is depicted as a powerful and benevolent healer.

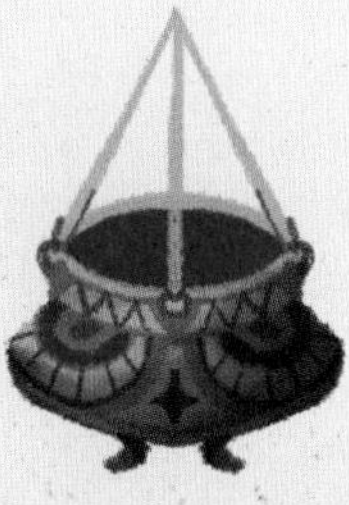

KING OBERON

OBERON IS A LEGENDARY FIGURE WHO APPEARS IN multiple instances of medieval lore, but it was Shakespeare's *A Midsummer Night's Dream* that turned him into a household name. King Oberon rules over the fairy realm with generosity and a sense of humor, but he is also known to be selfish and even cruel, using his power and status at times to seek his own end, regardless of how it affects others. In Shakespeare's play, Oberon casts a spell on his own wife, the fairy queen Titania, to trick her into handing over a boy who he wishes to make his servant. The spell makes his wife fall in love with a donkey's head.

THE MENEHUNE

ACCORDING TO HAWAI'IAN LEGEND, THE MENEHUNE are a group of small magical people who were the original settlers on the island of Kaua'i. They're known as exceptional craftsmen, building roads, ditches, temples, and other complex structures quickly and expertly using their magic. According to the legend, the Menehune left Kaua'i once humans began settling there, but some believe that a small group of them remain in Hawai'i today, building and crafting while evading human detection, as fairies are so good at doing.

THE JOGAH

THE JOGAH ARE SMALL SPIRIT-FOLK WHO ARE affiliated with the indigenous Mohawk, Cayuga, Tuscarora, and Seneca tribes. Descendants of the thunder god, Hinun, they are typically no taller than four feet and can turn invisible, though they have been known to reveal themselves to those who are in need. Different types of Jogah have appeared in Iroquois folklore, with various abilities like throwing stones down riverbanks or maintaining underground ecosystems. But what all the Jogah have in common is that they are all allies of the natural world and can affect the growth of crops, earthquakes, and so forth.

ALUXES

ALUXES ARE FAIRIES OF ANCIENT MAYAN TRADITION who are invisible to humans, though they will reveal themselves when they want something. Often, aluxes want something! These mischievous, chaos-loving fairies adore gifts. Farmers in the Yucatán Peninsula would leave offerings to aluxes, hoping to win their favor so that their crops might flourish that season. Aluxes can summon rain and protect your property at night, but only if they get something first.

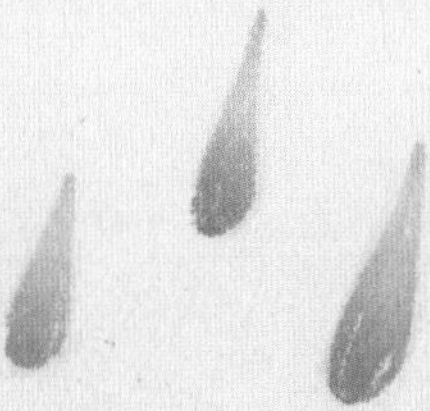

THE AOS SÍ

THE AOS SÍ ARE FAIRY FOLK WHOM SOME BELIEVE to be Celtic ancestors and who are known for their extreme beauty. Unlike other fairies, who are small in stature, the Aos Sí are described by many accounts as being at least as tall as humans. Neither troublemakers nor harbingers of good luck necessarily, the Aos Sí seem more neutral to humans than other fairies are, perhaps because they live in a separate world—an alternate universe, so to speak—that is permeable with ours only during certain periods of time. The door from their dimension to ours opens at dusk and closes again at dawn.

PATRONS OF THE BEES

THE THRIAE, ONE OF MANY TRIADS OF SISTERS from Greek mythology, were known as prophetics and are credited in Homeric texts with inventing the very art of divination, which they did by tossing stones. Melaina, Kleodora, and Daphnis lived in relation to the Greek gods but spent most of their time on Earth among nature. After all, they were the patrons of the bees and loved honey.

QUEEN TITANIA

TITANIA, A MEDIEVAL FAIRY QUEEN MADE FAMOUS by Shakespeare's *A Midsummer Night's Dream*, is known for being a powerful and often adversarial counterpart to her husband, King Oberon. Opinionated and stubborn, Queen Titania is not one to back down. She is ruled by her own ideas, whims, and desires, which cause tension and huge fights between her and her husband. In *A Midsummer Night's Dream*, Oberon resorts to magical foul play as a means of getting what he wants from her.

THE AZIZA

THE AZIZA ARE FAIRIES OF AFRICAN MYTHOLOGY who live in the forest, making homes on ant hills and silk-cotton trees. Unlike other fairies, who are eager to tease and sometimes trick humans, the Aziza are notoriously shy and keep to themselves for the most part. They have been described as beautiful and glowing with effervescent light.

YUMBOES

YUMBOES ARE FAIRIES OF SENEGALESE FOLKLORE who live beneath hills, where they enjoy throwing lavish feasts. Their banquets, which humans have been said to attend on occasion, are served by disembodied hands and feet. When they run out of food, the yumboes pay a visit to humans who are living nearby, taking what they need from pantries. In this way, yumboes are associated with the home and with family, some sources even saying they are the spirits of loved ones who have passed. They've been known to dance in the moonlight.

XANA

THE XANA IS A FAIRY OF ASTURIAN MYTHOLOGY, known for her breathtaking beauty and her association with water. In grottos, rivers, lakes, or anywhere there is fresh water, the xana guards her treasure and combs her long hair with a gold or silver comb said to be made out of light from the sun or moon. This water fairy is kind to humans and has been known to give them gifts, sometimes in gold.

FOX FAIRIES

THE HULI JING OF CHINESE FOLKLORE ARE FOX spirits whose shape-shifting powers grow stronger as they age. With resonances in Japan and Korea as the kitsune and kumiho respectively, the huli jing most often take the form of young women who lure men to death using powers of seduction. In order to stay immortal, the huli jing feed on human life. Older huli jing were expert shape-shifters and could turn into men and women, old and young.

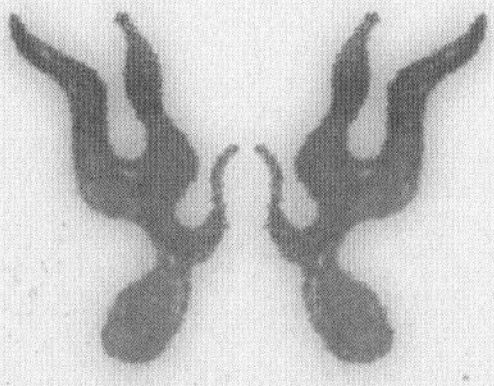

WATER DEITIES

IN JAPANESE FOLKLORE, THE KAPPA ARE WATER deities who inhabit the rivers and ponds of Japan. With scales and webbed fingers, these magical reptilian creatures embody many different qualities that reveal juxtaposing values. Morally ambiguous, they can be terrorizing at times, stealing livestock and even children, but they're also known as respectful to a fault, bowing so low that they spill the bowl of water indented into their heads, thereby losing the source of their powers. Good on their word, if you help a kappa refill the water, they will be indebted to you and will fulfill whatever promise they make.

PUCK

THE CHARACTER PUCK OF MEDIEVAL ENGLISH folklore is a fairy who can be summarized in one word: naughty. In earlier depictions, he was portrayed as malicious, the Old English word *puck* meaning demon. But later literature would reveal a much more playful rather than cruel fairy who liked gifts and would bestow good fortune upon those who left him offerings. A domestic fairy, he's been known to steal stuff around the house. In Shakespeare's *A Midsummer Night's Dream*, Puck is characterized as King Oberon's loyal sidekick and assists the fairy king in making Titania, the fairy queen, fall in love with a donkey's head.

BANSHEE

A BANSHEE IS A FAIRY OF CELTIC FOLKLORE WHO is known for wailing loudly into the night to warn of imminent death. Sources say that if someone heard the scream, their loved one would soon pass. Some believed that each family had its own banshee who would foretell of grief ahead. The screams have been described as shrill and terrifying, as one can imagine a sign of death would be.

JINN

IN ARABIC FOLKLORE, JINN ARE SHAPE-SHIFTING beings who have incredible powers that enable them to either help or harm humans. They're said to take on many forms, including those of animals, humans, and even smoke, their bodies being made from fire. The jinn who appear in the Qu'ran are depicted as having the ability to discern clearly between right and wrong. These supernatural beings also show up in the canonical *One Thousand and One Nights* as sometimes vengeful and sometimes kind characters, granting wishes to those in need.

TINKER BELL

TINKER BELL MIGHT JUST BE THE MOST POPULAR fairy of all time, thanks to the Disney animated classic based on the original play *Peter Pan*, by Sir James M. Barry. She is named after the sound she made, like tinkering bells, and after her role of fixing pots and kettles. Adored for her feisty personality, Tinker Bell is emotional and can act childish at times, drawn by the seat of her whims. She is Peter Pan's companion on his adventures in Neverland.

MOUNT OF
JUPITER
MOUNT OF
SATURN
MOUNT OF
APOLLO
MOUNT OF
MERCURY
THE HEART LINE
THE HEAD LINE
INNER MOUNT OF MARS
OUTER MOUNT OF MARS
THE LIFE LINE
THE LINE OF FATE
MOUNT OF
VENUS
MOUNT OF THE
MOON

CHAPTER 3

PALMISTRY

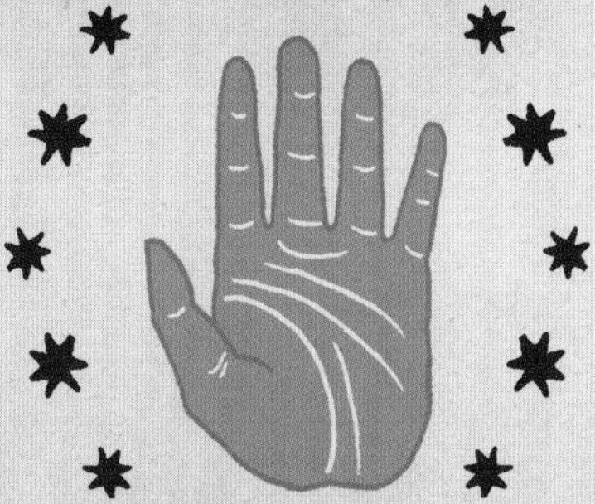

Palmistry—also called palm reading, chiromancy, and chirology—is one of the oldest and best-known divination practices in the world. It's a deceptively simple concept based on the beliefs that the physical characteristics of one's hand correspond to their personality and life path and that one can gain insight into their character and fate by closely studying their palms and fingers.

Though the exact genesis of palm reading remains shrouded in mystery, those who study the practice most commonly believe it to have originated in India thousands of years ago and subsequently spread to China,

Egypt, Persia, and Greece, and then to other countries in Europe. In antiquity, the practice was widespread and influential, referenced directly by Aristotle and mentioned in the Book of Job. Although it was banned by the Catholic Church during the Middle Ages, the practice experienced a revival in the 19th century as interest in the occult grew. Nowadays, the concept of palm reading is widespread in pop culture—but few people actually know how it works.

So what, exactly, does palmistry entail, and how can you start to practice it at home? Full mastery can take years and requires an in-depth understanding of the shapes, lines, and tactile qualities of the palm. But don't get intimidated: It's easy to do a simple reading if you know the basics!

To start, you should look at the querent's dominant hand, the one they use for writing. This is called the Active hand, and it's associated with someone's near future, their plans, and the self they've acquired during their journey through life—their present circumstances and direction, in essence. (You can also read the non-dominant hand, known as the Inactive hand, if you'd like; it's linked with someone's potential, their longer-term plans, and their innate strengths and weaknesses.)

Look at the hand. What is it shaped like? How do the lines appear—are they deep or shallow? Curved or straight? What does the palm feel like to the touch? Once you've familiarized yourself with the energy of the palm, you can begin identifying certain notable characteristics: the shape of the palm; the four main lines: heart, head, life, and fate; and the mounts, or fleshy bumps, at the base of the fingers and around the palm.

THE FOUR HAND SHAPES

There are four basic hand shapes in palmistry, each of which corresponds with one of the four classical elements: fire, water, earth, and air. (If you're familiar with astrology, you'll know that the zodiac signs are divided into these four elements as well.)

Each hand shape has its own personality profile. To figure out which one you're looking at, compare the proportions of the palm to the length of the fingers. A palm is considered "short" or "square" if it's about as wide as it is long; a "long" palm is more rectangular in shape, longer than it is wide. If the fingers are about the same length as the palm, they're considered "long"; if they're any shorter than the palm, they're considered "short."

Keep in mind that palm reading is an interplay between the reader and the hand: If some of these measurements seem subjective, that's because they're meant to be open to interpretation. The longer you practice palmistry, the more comfortable you'll get with making these designations, using your intuition as much as your powers of observation.

FIRE HANDS have long palms and short fingers. The palms may be a bit fleshy, and they're known for having quite distinct, deeply etched lines, as well as easily distinguishable mounts. People with fire hands are said to be creative, passionate, and a bit impulsive. They're magnetic and compelling but can lack tact, and they tend to get restless easily.

WATER HANDS are recognizable by their long, rectangular palms and long fingers. Their lines tend to be finely etched, and their hands may feel clammy to the touch. People with water hands are nurturing, empathetic, intuitive, and naturally artistic. They're prone to oversensitivity, though, and can get swallowed up in other people's problems or their own fantasy worlds.

EARTH HANDS display short, square palms and short fingers. Their skin may feel a little coarse, and they might have fewer lines—though those that do show up will be deeply etched. Individuals with earth hands are practical, grounded, and down-to-earth. They're hardworking and reliable but can get so absorbed in the day-to-day that they forget to focus on the big picture.

AIR HANDS have short palms and long fingers, which may appear spindly or bony; they also tend to have dry skin. They're naturally intelligent, charming, and gifted at communication, but they're easily distracted and can grow anxious when not provided with constant stimulation.

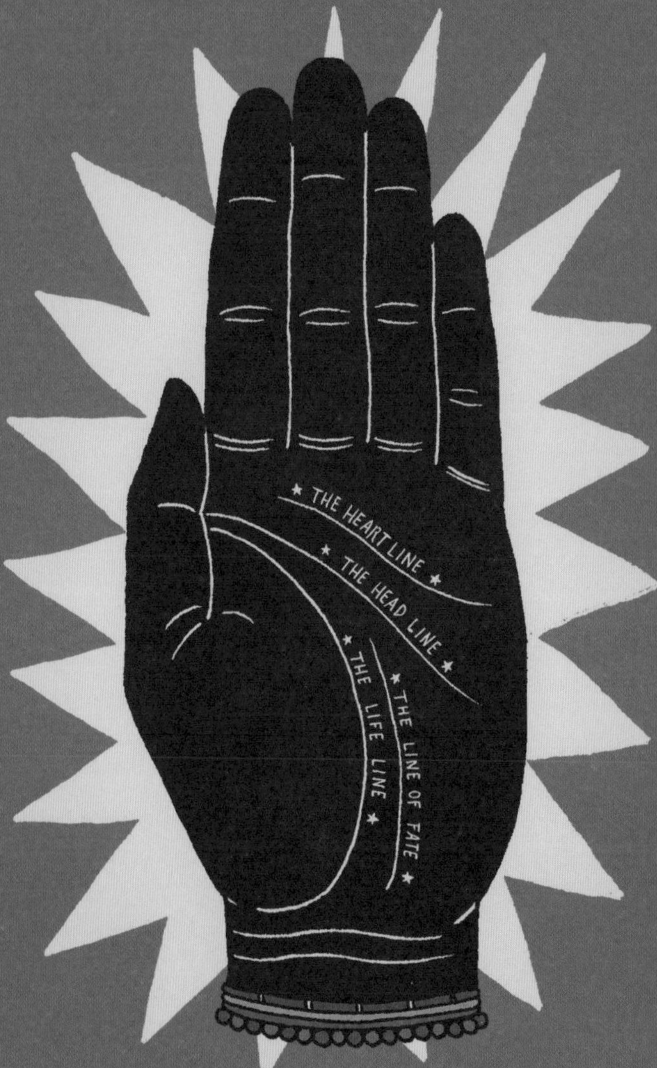
★ THE HEART LINE ★
★ THE HEAD LINE ★
★ THE LIFE LINE ★
★ THE LINE OF FATE ★

THE LINES

You're probably already familiar with the concept of a "life line" because it's referenced constantly in pop-culture depictions of palm reading. But this is only one of several lines you can consult in your reading; each provides insight into a specific area of life.

There are four major lines on every hand: the heart line, the head line, the life line, and the line of fate or destiny.

THE HEART LINE is the line that appears at the very top of the palm, beneath the fingers; it starts at or near the pinky and ends beneath the middle or index finger. It's associated with our emotional state, our relationships and friendships, and our sexuality—anything that pertains to the heart.

The depth of this line corresponds to the intensity of one's emotions and emotional experiences, and the length reveals how extroverted the person is: A short heart line may indicate that someone values alone time, whereas someone with a long heart line may be more likely to seek out relationships and thrive in the company of others.

If the line is dramatically curved, that can indicate that a person is very passionate and driven by their emotions, whereas a flat, straight line can show that someone is more practical and rational and may even come across as aloof.

A break in the heart line can indicate the end of a relationship, multiple lovers, or infidelity.

✷•✷•✷

THE HEAD LINE is just below the heart line, running from the space between the thumb and index finger to the fleshy area between and beneath the ring finger and the pinky. It may intersect with the heart line at its origin, or it could also intersect with the life line—every palm is different!

The head line is associated with one's thoughts and intellect and areas of intellectual curiosity. It can also reveal the areas in life where lessons will be learned. A deeper line indicates strong interest in intellectual pursuits, whereas a shallow line indicates that the person is not particularly interested in higher learning or overanalyzing things. The length of the line corresponds to the breadth of subjects a person will study in their lifetime: If it's shorter, the person may be more focused on one specific topic, while someone with a long head line may be more of a generalist or a specialist in multiple fields.

A break in the head line could indicate confusion or a crisis of faith or, alternatively, a life-changing epiphany.

THE LIFE LINE frames the thumb in a semicircle shape, starting between the thumb and the index finger and ending on or near the wrist. If you see a short life line, don't panic! The life line doesn't actually indicate how long someone will live but rather their passion, vitality, and enthusiasm. The depth of the line is associated with the intensity of one's life experiences, and the length reflects how independent they are: Someone with a short life line is likely to be self-motivated and autonomous, whereas a longer life line may reflect more of a team player who has a tendency to rely on others and work cooperatively.

A long, unbroken life line can indicate a smooth passage through life with little conflict or stress. A sudden break is associated with crisis or rapid change, but that's not necessarily a bad thing—sudden, drastic change can bring excitement and inspiration, after all.

THE LINE OF FATE OR DESTINY starts at the base of the palm and extends up toward the middle finger. It can take myriad different forms. If it's long and straight, dividing the palm and stretching well toward the middle finger, that can indicate a clear, sure life path with few interruptions. If the fate line is short and indistinct, the person may have to spend some time exploring their options before settling on their life path. It's possible that the fate line may be absent altogether; this means that the person may have to make their own destiny.

Of all the lines on the palm, this one is the most prone to changing over time. Sometimes a fate line will appear in the middle of one's life, and it can also grow or fade as one ages. If you encounter a fate line that's faint and indistinct, that doesn't mean the person is doomed to an aimless life or that their path is wavering—instead, it can be read as a sign that an important decision needs to be made so that their path can become clear.

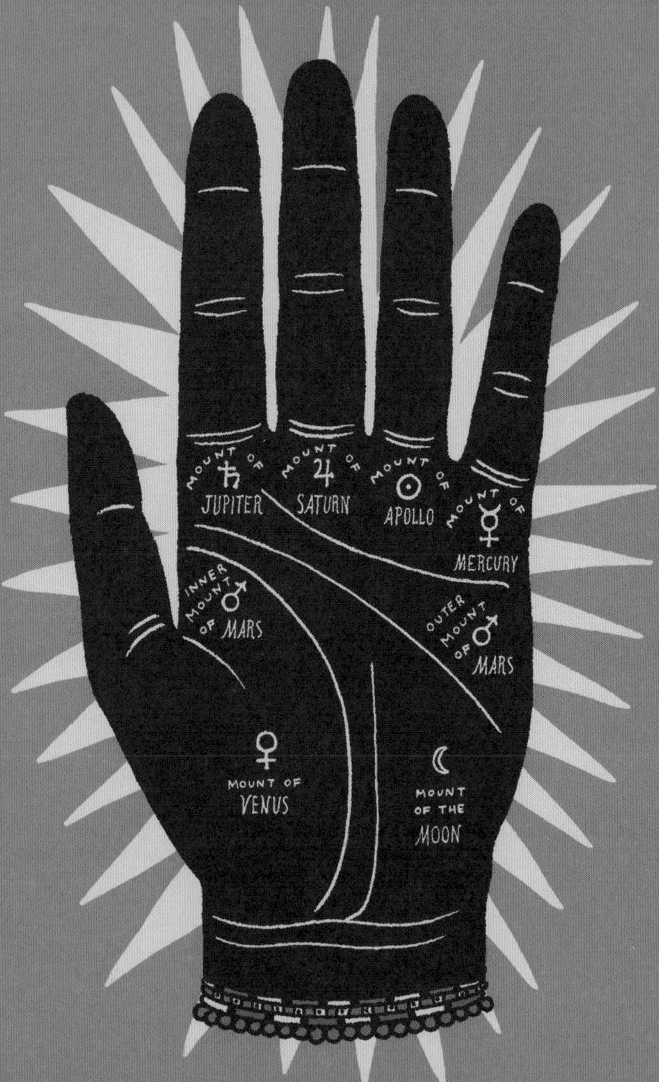
MOUNT OF
JUPITER
MOUNT OF
SATURN
MOUNT OF
APOLLO
MOUNT OF
MERCURY
INNER MOUNT OF MARS
OUTER MOUNT OF MARS
MOUNT OF
VENUS
MOUNT OF THE
MOON

THE MOUNTS

Every hand has seven main mounts, which are fleshy, raised areas beneath the fingers and on the periphery of the palm. These correspond to the seven main celestial bodies in classical astrology: We have the mounts of Apollo (the sun), the moon, Mercury, Venus, Mars, Jupiter, and Saturn.

Each of these corresponds to a specific characteristic. If a mount is prominent and well-developed, that quality may manifest strongly in someone's personality. If it's small and hard to discern, that quality may be underdeveloped or repressed. If a mount is incredibly prominent, that could indicate that its corresponding quality is exaggerated or excessive.

THE MOUNT OF JUPITER is located at the base of the index finger. It's associated with confidence, ambition, and leadership, as well as altruism, idealism, and wisdom. Someone with a firm, high mount of Jupiter might be a natural leader and mentor, eager to share their wisdom and help those less fortunate. An underdeveloped mount of Jupiter could indicate that someone tends to prefer following others and may struggle with confidence. An overly large mount of Jupiter is associated with having a big ego or being a know-it-all or ruthless in the quest for power and acclaim.

* 4 *

THE MOUNT OF SATURN is located beneath the middle finger; it tends to be flatter than the others. It's associated with responsibility and how one copes with problems. If it's overdeveloped, that can indicate that a person is rigid, stubborn, and resistant to change. A well-developed mount of Saturn might mean that the individual has healthy boundaries and handles adversity well; if the mount is completely flat, the person may be indecisive and anxious.

THE MOUNT OF APOLLO is located under the ring finger, and it corresponds to creativity, artistic ability, charisma, good fortune, and sense of optimism. If it's prominent and well-developed, the individual is likely to be creative, concerned with aesthetics, magnetic, and lucky. A flat mount of Apollo is associated with lack of imagination and a tendency to be overly critical; a person with this quality may tend to overrely on data and facts.

THE MOUNT OF MERCURY is located beneath the pinky, and it's related to communication, intelligence, and wit. If it's large and well-formed, the individual is likely to be communicative and sharp, good at expressing their ideas and keeping in touch with others. A small and underdeveloped mount of Mercury is linked to shyness and trouble communicating.

THE OUTER MOUNT OF MARS is located directly under the mount of Mercury, in the middle third of the palm under the pinky. It represents courage, self-control, and the ability to push forward. A well-developed mount of Mars will be firm to the touch and will manifest in strong opinions and a strong will. A flat mount of Mars is associated with timidity. If the mount is overdeveloped, an individual might be aggressive, unreasonable, and overly assertive.

THE INNER MOUNT OF MARS is located across the palm, between the thumb and the index finger, below the mount of Jupiter. Its meaning is similar: It's related to moral courage and the ability to stand up for one's beliefs.

THE MOUNT OF THE MOON is located beneath the mount of Mercury, just above the wrist, extending to the end of the hand. It's the largest mount on the palm and usually very fleshy. It's associated with intuition, the subconscious, and imaginative power. Someone with a well-developed mount of the moon could be psychically gifted, sensitive, and intuitive, with an active imagination; conversely, if the mount is small, the individual may prefer familiar experiences and feel safer following instructions. An overdeveloped mount of the moon is associated with overindulging in fantasies and daydreams and feeling disconnected from reality.

THE MOUNT OF VENUS is located under the thumb, right across from the mount of the moon; it's also quite large, stretching to the edge of the hand. Like its namesake, the planet of love and beauty, it is associated with sexual passion, sensuality, love, and attraction. If the mount of Venus is fleshy and pronounced, the individual is likely to be sensual, romantic, and drawn to beauty and luxury; if it's overly prominent, the person may be prone to overindulging and overspending. A mount of Venus that feels flat or hollow is associated with a low sex drive or a fear of romantic involvement.

GO FORTH

Once you've gotten these basics down, you're ready to start palm reading on your own. But keep in mind that this is just the surface level of the craft—there's much more to learn, should you be interested. You should also remember that the lines on one's palm don't spell out an absolute destiny. They're merely indications of what might happen should a person continue down the same path. Just like our individual destinies, the mounts and lines of a palm are subject to change as we live; that's one of the reasons palmistry is so rewarding and complex!

THE DEVIL
THE HANGED MAN
THE TOWER
STRENGTH
DEATH
THE MOON
THE EMPRESS
THE LOVERS
THE STAR
WHEEL of FORTUNE
JUSTICE
THE FOOL
THE HIG

CHAPTER 4

TAROT

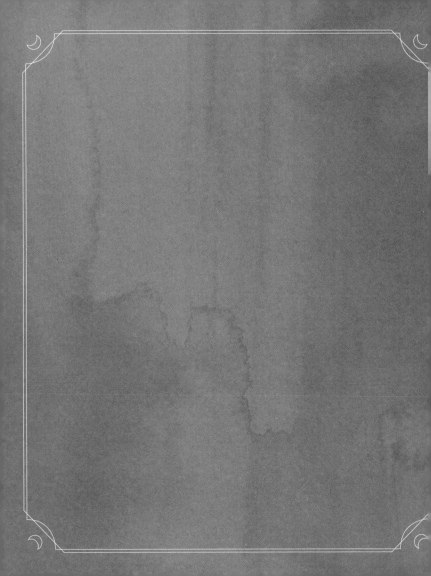

Tarot cards started out as cards for games—and much like the playing cards we use today, there are four suits, with aces, kings, queens, and all the way down to deuces. It wasn't until the late 1700s that tarot came to mean what it does today: a form of divination. Now, that's a fairly confusing term—does divination really allow you to see the future?

No, not *really*. Just as fortune cookies don't really tell your fortune, tarot cards are not magical windows that allow you to see what is to come. But, every once in a while, when you go out for Chinese takeout you'll get a fortune cookie with a message that is eerily spot-on. It will seem to be speaking to you personally, talking about the way you move through the world.

Tarot works much the same way—only in this case, it happens *all* the time, not just once in a while when you get a good cookie. The thing about tarot is, it's always accurate because it's always telling you what you already know. If that doesn't seem particularly useful, think about it this way—when you do a tarot reading, you will often feel a sense of relief, a confirmation that what you believed deep down to be true is, in fact, true. Tarot cards can reveal to you what you know

instinctively, intuitively, but maybe haven't quite allowed yourself to accept. Sometimes we look away from the hard truths, or we don't allow ourselves to see the possibilities of our wildest dreams. Tarot pulls the secrets you hide from yourself up from your depths and lays them in front of you.

But no harm can come to you from a bunch of pieces of paper—and that's all these cards ultimately are. They can help you face what you've been avoiding, and they can help you understand what it is you truly want. They help you to know yourself. And best of all, they can give you advice! When you don't know what to do next, tarot cards will lead the way—guiding you as you navigate your own instincts, helping you walk carefully over the stepping stones that lead you to where you truly want to go.

THE CARDS

While there are four suits in tarot, they aren't Diamonds, Hearts, Clubs, and Spades. Instead, tarot moves through Cups, Pentacles, Swords, and Wands. Each of these suits has a specific meaning, an area of life that it governs and can give you information about. All of the cards that fall within the suits are known as the Minor Arcana. You'll notice a pattern within the Minor Arcana—for instance, the eighth card in each suit represents some form of struggle—and you'll see that they flow from beginnings to endings. But there is never truly an ending in tarot, as we are all always learning, evolving, and growing.

✦CUPS✦

Every suit is ruled by an element, and Cups are ruled by water. Water is mysterious, flowing, and difficult to contain. It sustains life, but it can also be destructive.

The suit of Cups is the suit of relationships. It's about the people who fill our lives and how we feel about them. This suit is dominated by emotion—so any choices offered by Cups will be choices made from the heart rather than with the logic of the mind. That can sound like a good thing—we're always being told to listen to our hearts!—but it can have its downside. We don't want to make choices based *entirely* in emotion; it's important to use our heads, as well.

ACE. The Ace of Cups represents a new, blossoming relationship.

TWO. The Two of Cups stands for unity, for attraction and intimacy.

THREE. The Three of Cups is a joyous card, celebrating friendship and cooperation.

FOUR. The Four of Cups takes a sharp downward turn, pulling away from those you love, feeling apathy and self-absorption.

FIVE. The downward spiral continues with the Five of Cups, as you feel regret or grief over a failure.

SIX. The Six of Cups looks back, nostalgic for childhood and a more innocent time.

SEVEN. The Seven of Cups represents a chance to begin again, with new choices and opportunities—but also new temptations.

EIGHT. The Eight of Cups appears when things did not work out. You feel dissatisfied and disappointed.

NINE. The Nine of Cups, on the other hand, represents utter bliss and fulfillment.

TEN. The Ten of Cups is just what we want in our relationships—they are happy and healthy, particularly familial relationships.

PAGE. The Page of Cups is full of potential, of childlike curiosity and possibility.

KNIGHT. The Knight of Cups is a romantic, but he tends to live in a bit of a fantasy world.

QUEEN. The Queen of Cups is nurturing and in touch with her intuition.

KING. The King of Cups is mature and full of excellent advice. Unlike the rest of this suit, he is able to balance logic and emotion.

PENTACLES

The element of Pentacles is earth, and as such, it's a very practical suit. It governs our basic needs and goals, and it is the suit of work and prosperity. This can mean your job or the work you do around the home, but generally speaking we're talking about monetary gain. This may seem shallow, particularly for something as whimsical as tarot, but think about it—how would you be able to support your relationships, your creativity, and your heart if you didn't feel safe and secure? Pentacles are just as important a suit as any other.

That said, you definitely don't want to get caught up in focusing on Pentacles alone, or you may lose sight of what means the most to you.

ACE. The Ace of Pentacles represents the potential for financial abundance, perhaps a new career opportunity.

TWO. When the Two of Pentacles appears, it means you are able to prioritize and work efficiently.

THREE. Things are moving forward with the Three of Pentacles, as you collaborate and get organized.

FOUR. Unfortunately, the Four of Pentacles calls this progression to a halt. It's time to be frugal.

FIVE. With the Five of Pentacles, things get even worse—isolation, worry, and monetary concerns are looming.

SIX. The Six of Pentacles is a gift of generosity, as in one you receive from others.

SEVEN. The Seven of Pentacles means it's time to assess—should you persevere and invest more in your current project?

EIGHT. With the Eight of Pentacles, it's time to buckle down. You're going to be working hard for a while, but it will be worth it in the end.

NINE. And with the Nine of Pentacles, it is worth it—you have achieved success and self-sufficiency.

TEN. The Ten of Pentacles looks at long-term abundance, wealth, and stability.

PAGE. The Page of Pentacles is motivated, capable, and excited to learn new skills.

KNIGHT. The Knight of Pentacles is productive, hardworking, and focused.

QUEEN. Think of the Queen of Pentacles as a working mom—she is nurturing, yet practical.

KING. The King of Pentacles is a confident leader, particularly in business.

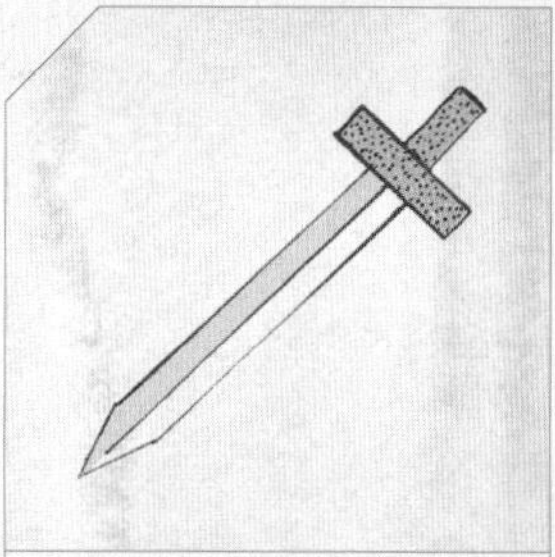

✶ SWORDS ✶

Swords are ruled by the element of air. While that may seem a little flighty for such a sharp suit, think about the clarity and necessity of air. Aptly enough, the suit of Swords covers any conflicts you may have in your life, usually when the mind is at war with the heart. Swords help you cut through your emotions with logic. If that sounds cold and harsh, know that it's sometimes necessary. Swords can allow us to see what's really going on, including truths we may be hiding from ourselves.

ACE. The Ace of Swords represents a breakthrough of new ideas.

TWO. When the Two of Swords appears, you are facing a difficult decision that you have been avoiding.

THREE. The Three of Swords is a painful card, full of heartbreak.

FOUR. The Four of Swords is a time of rest and recovery.

FIVE. The Five of Swords indicates a defeat, and an ugly one. You may feel some resentment.

SIX. The Six of Swords allows you to let go and transition to a new outlook.

SEVEN. The Seven of Swords is a card of strategy, but be careful, because strategy can easily turn into manipulation.

EIGHT. The Eight of Swords indicates that you are suffering from self-doubt. You feel that you don't have any good choices—but this may be because of your own limiting beliefs.

NINE. The Nine of Swords appears when you're feeling anxious and afraid, even depressed.

TEN. The Ten of Swords means you're in crisis. Prepare for an ordeal.

PAGE. The Page of Swords is a seeker, always looking for knowledge and new perspectives.

KNIGHT. The Knight of Swords is ambitious and assertive, but he doesn't always think ahead.

QUEEN. The Queen of Swords is not a sentimental woman. She sets firm boundaries and isn't afraid of hard truths.

KING. The King of Swords is a powerful intellectual authority. Listen to his advice.

✴ WANDS ✴

The element of Wands is fire, the power to strike a spark of creativity. Wands are energetic and intuitive, pushing you to expand and become whatever you most desire. They push at your boundaries and urge you to allow your true self to shine free. Wands are definitely the most exciting and inspiring suit . . . but there is a danger here. If you pursue Wands to the detriment of the other suits, you may burn in your own creative fire, having lost sight of the practical, the logical, and the loving parts of your life, like the people who matter most to you. Listen to what Wands have to say, for they speak about your creative desires, but don't let them shout at you and drown out everything else.

ACE. The Ace of Wands is enthusiastic, bursting with creativity.

TWO. The Two of Wands represents the planning stage of an idea, as you set some goals.

THREE. The Three of Wands represents progress, as you begin to share your idea with others.

FOUR. It's time to celebrate! The Four of Wands indicates an early success, so sit back, rest, and take it in.

FIVE. Some roadblocks appear with the Five of Wands, as you face some opposition and conflicting opinions.

SIX. Another success with the Six of Wands! Bask in your self-confidence—you deserve it.

SEVEN. You may be facing some competition when the Seven of Wands appears. Persevere and protect your process.

EIGHT. With the Eight of Wands, it's time to shift quickly into action.

NINE. The Nine of Wands tells you to hold on to your resilience. You are strong and capable.

TEN. With the Ten of Wands, you reach a sense of completion. You feel responsible and committed.

PAGE. The Page of Wands is a free spirit, curious and on a journey of discovery.

KNIGHT. The Knight of Wands is energetic and passionate, but can be a little impulsive.

QUEEN. The powerful Queen of Wands is determined and courageous.

KING. The King of Wands is a man of vision. He sees the big picture and knows how to make it happen.

THE MAJOR ARCANA

0 **THE FOOL.** The Fool represents the pure wisdom and innocence of childhood, along with the potential for growth.

1 **THE MAGICIAN.** The Magician is skilled and capable, a powerful high-achiever.

2 **THE HIGH PRIESTESS.** The High Priestess is the feminine alternative to the Magician. Equally powerful, but with a more mystical, mysterious, and intuitive presence.

3 **THE EMPRESS.** The Empress is loving and sensuous. She is nurturing, creative, and fertile.

4 **THE EMPEROR.** The Emperor is a just and fair leader, but his authority comes from tradition, and as such he can be overly structured.

5 **THE HIEROPHANT.** The Hierophant represents your established belief system, whether that is religious, social, academic, or political.

6 THE LOVERS. The Lovers may refer to a literal romantic relationship, but it can also mean an easy, peaceful marriage of two disparate parts within yourself.

7 THE CHARIOT. The Chariot is about the work that goes into finding a balance between two opposing parts.

8 STRENGTH. This card is about strength in the long term, to get through a difficult situation over time—and do it well.

9 THE HERMIT. The Hermit is the introvert's favorite card. It asks you to take some time to contemplate, to step back from a situation so you can gain some clarity.

10 WHEEL OF FORTUNE. The Wheel of Fortune asks you to believe in something more, that there is a force for good in the world, guiding you through good times and bad.

11 JUSTICE. Justice represents fairness, truth, and karma.

12 **THE HANGED MAN.** The Hanged Man is about the sacrifices we must make in search of knowledge, self-awareness, and truth.

13 **DEATH.** Death does not mean literal death, but instead a change or an ending, the death of a way of being or approaching the world.

14 **TEMPERANCE.** When Temperance appears, it's a sign that you shouldn't rush into anything. Take a moment to listen to what others have to say and think things through.

15 **THE DEVIL.** The Devil is almost always the devil within—when you are your own worst enemy. Self-deception, destructive impulses, and self-sabotage are rearing their heads.

16 **THE TOWER.** If Death is about change, the Tower is about starting over completely, but on the other side of this painful change you'll find peace.

17 **THE STAR.** The Star is about new beginnings. Think of a star born of a nebula formed by a collapsed star, renewing again and again.

18 **THE MOON.** The Moon speaks to our illusions, our unconscious fears. In the moonlight, things can look unreal and therefore scary—but there really isn't anything to fear.

19 **THE SUN.** The Sun represents clarity, confidence, and positivity. Now you can see what's really going on and feel sure about your path.

20 **JUDGMENT.** Judgment is your opportunity to look back and evaluate the choices you have made, knowing that nothing is final—you can always choose differently.

21 **THE WORLD.** When the World appears, it is telling you that you have done what you wanted to do, or you soon will if you follow the path.

HOW TO DO A READING

The descriptions of the meanings of each card are just archetypes, offering history and grounding to your reading, and giving you a place to start. But as you work with tarot, you will begin to add your own meanings to the cards, based on your own experiences, intuitions, and connections—and as you do this, tarot will take you further and have more to offer, showing you a deeper meaning and giving you greater clarity. Always start by shuffling your cards—or having the person you're reading for shuffle them—and then hold the cards close to your heart and ask them for guidance.

There are so many different spreads available in tarot. These are three common ones that are easy to work with.

THREE-CARD SPREAD

This spread is deceptively simple, as it offers so much information with just a few cards. Once you've shuffled, fan the cards out in a line so that each card is visible, face down. If a certain card seems to want to stay hidden, let it. Choose three cards, and let your intuition guide you. If the answer to your question seems hidden from you, perhaps choose a hidden card. Sometimes your card will make your fingers tingle, or it might feel slightly warm beneath your hands.

Lay your three chosen cards face up. Interpret them from left to right. They may represent the past, the present, and the future, or you may read them as your conscious, your unconscious, and what is most alive for you today, in this moment.

GUIDANCE SPREAD

This spread can be useful when you're facing a particular challenge or having trouble seeing all sides of a complicated issue. With this spread, you'll draw eight cards, placing the first card off to one side, and the following seven cards in a row all together.

1. This card represents your primary concern, the issue at hand.

2. What's your motivation? Why are you looking for guidance here?

3. This card represents the area(s) in your life that you feel anxious about.

4. This card points out elements in your situation that you may not be aware of.

5. This card will give you the information you require in order to overcome your apprehensions.

---

6. This card will help you feel comfortable letting your anxieties go.

---

7. This card will advise you on how to move forward.

---

8. This card tells you how it could all work out in the end, if you follow the path.

CELTIC CROSS

The Celtic Cross is a classic tarot spread, and it's so popular because it's incredibly useful—it can help you find the answer to any question, no matter how complex. Remember, nothing tarot can tell you will be anything you don't already know, deep down.

1. This card represents you, how you are at this moment in time. What is going on with you? What are you experiencing, and how are you reacting to that experience?

---

2. Crossing the first card is the second; this card literally represents whatever is crossing you, whatever in your life is running antithetical to what you want and who you are.

---

3. What has happened in the past to create this situation?

---

4. This card represents the immediate future—it is not the resolution of the situation, but it can give you some idea as to what will happen next.

---

5. What do you want? What are your goals? What do you believe is the right thing for your situation?

---

6. The sixth card questions the answers given by the fifth. Perhaps that was only what you *think* you want, or believe to be right. What does your intuition, your subconscious think? Are they in agreement?

---

7. What are your best next steps? This card will advise you.

8. The eighth card reminds you that you can only control what *you* do. There are external influences represented here, and they can have an impact on the situation, too.

9. This card speaks to your hopes and fears. It can often be difficult to interpret, since the two are frequently intertwined. Look back to the answers given in the sixth card, and see how the two relate.

10. The resolution. How will this situation play out? What will happen in the end? If the answer given by this card is not the one you want, know that you have the power to change it. If you keep on your current course, this is what will happen. This card will tell you if you need to take a different path.

CHAPTER 5

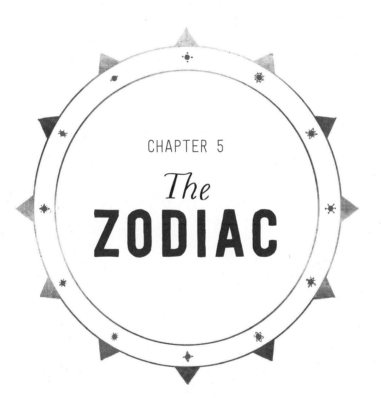

The ZODIAC

IN WESTERN ASTROLOGY, THE ZODIAC COMPRISES A BAND of twelve constellations, which the sun, the moon, and the planets move through over the course of a year. Each of these constellations represents a particular Sign of the zodiac, and each Sign is ruled by a particular celestial body (the sun, the moon, Venus, and so forth). Astrology has been around since long before our modern calendar, so the Signs follow the seasons, rather than the calendar year, with spring coming first—because of that, the month of the first Sign of the zodiac, Aries, begins with the Spring Equinox. In order, the Signs are Aries, Taurus, Gemini, Cancer, Leo, Virgo, Libra, Scorpio, Sagittarius, Capricorn, Aquarius, and Pisces.

The Signs fall into the elemental categories of fire, water, earth, and air. Although each Sign is distinct from any other, Signs within an elemental category tend to have several traits in common, and they tend to get along with one other.

FIRE SIGNS • *ARIES, LEO, and SAGITTARIUS are all powerful, energetic, and vibrant. They tend to be creative and charismatic, and people are often drawn to them. They are passionate and feel their emotions deeply.*

EARTH SIGNS • *TAURUS, VIRGO, and CAPRICORN are responsible and hardworking. They get things done. They are loyal and patient, and, generally speaking, don't like to take risks. That said, they can be very ambitious and often find a way of getting what they want in life.*

AIR SIGNS • *GEMINI, LIBRA, and AQUARIUS are all very smart—but they are also impulsive and quickly drawn to the next thing that interests them. They have a great deal of curiosity and are engaged by a variety of topics. They are social, excel at communication, and value truth and balance.*

WATER SIGNS • *CANCER, SCORPIO, and PISCES can be somewhat unpredictable, partly because they are ruled by their emotions. They are sensitive, intuitive, and empathetic, and they use these qualities to fuel their imaginations.*

What's Your Sign? Well, It's Complicated

WE MAY THINK WE KNOW OUR SIGN. WE GET OUR DAILY horoscope in a brief paragraph, and we use the Signs as shorthand for personality types. This can be quite useful—but it's just the beginning. The truth is that what we think of as "our Sign" is just one of the many aspects of personality and self that astrology covers. Our birth Sign is usually our Sun Sign, meaning the constellation that the sun was moving through at the time we were born. But that's not the whole picture.

SUN SIGN • *Your Sun Sign is your basic nature, the parts of yourself that remain constant no matter what is going on in your life.*

MOON SIGN • *Your Moon Sign is determined by which constellation the moon was moving through at the time you were born. It indicates your emotions, your innermost thoughts, and your moods.*

ASCENDANT OR RISING SIGN • *Your Rising Sign is determined by which constellation was just coming up over the horizon at the time of your birth. It represents the part of yourself that you present to the world.*

Each of these Signs is equally important in astrology. Only by interpreting them together, in conversation with one another, can we truly understand our own nature—which will allow us to move with intention as we harness the power and information the zodiac can provide.

The Planetary Bodies

JUST AS THE CONSTELLATIONS MOVE, SO DO THE PLANETARY bodies, which move through them. Each planetary body has its own energy, and when it is within a certain Sign, its energy infuses that Sign. This is useful information! If you know that the passion of Venus or the clarity and communication of Mercury is coming your way, you can plan accordingly.

SUN • *The Sun provides us with light and life. It represents ego, health, and pride, particularly in ourselves. The Sun makes it journey through the zodiac once per year, spending about a month with each Sign.*

MOON • *The Moon represents our intuition, our deepest feelings, and our private lives. It's connected to our ancestors and helps us get in touch with our emotions. The Moon takes only twenty-eight days to travel through the zodiac, spending two to three days with each Sign.*

MERCURY • *Mercury is all about communication. Research, learning, decision-making, persuasion—all of these actions fall in the realm of Mercury. When Mercury goes retrograde (meaning when it appears to be moving backward across the night sky), all of this goes haywire. Technology doesn't work, lines of communication fall apart, and, generally speaking, everything is just a little* off. *Mercury spends about a month in each Sign as it travels across the zodiac.*

VENUS • *Venus represents love, beauty, and pleasure. Impulsivity and a lack of consequences can come into play with this planet, but Venus can also help us learn what we truly love, enjoy, and value. Venus generally takes around eleven months to travel across the zodiac, spending a few weeks with each Sign.*

MARS • *Mars is aggressive, energetic, competitive, and brave. Mars is the energy of conflict, whether that is actual war, arguments, or even just sports. If this feels uncomfortable, know that sometimes a little of Mars' confidence and energy can be a good thing. Mars takes approximately two years to circle the zodiac, spending six or seven weeks with each Sign.*

JUPITER • *Jupiter is a planet of wisdom and faith. It asks us to expand our knowledge and awareness, to learn new things—for it is only when we recognize what we do* not *know that we can become truly wise. Jupiter takes twelve years to travel the zodiac, and it sits with each Sign for a full year.*

SATURN • *Saturn urges caution and responsibility. Its energy is mature and patient, suggesting structure, forethought, and realism. Saturn takes twenty-nine years to go across the zodiac and stays in each Sign for two and a half years.*

URANUS • *Uranus rules the future, particularly technology. Innovation and experimentation—these are Uranus' favorite things. Uranus takes eighty-four years to circle the zodiac and stays with a Sign for seven of those years—so you can expect a lot of creativity during those seven years.*

NEPTUNE • *Neptune is mysterious. Like the moon, it governs dreams, intuition, and the subconscious. But unlike the moon, it stays with you for years—fourteen years in fact—making that period of your life a time of true inner transformation.*

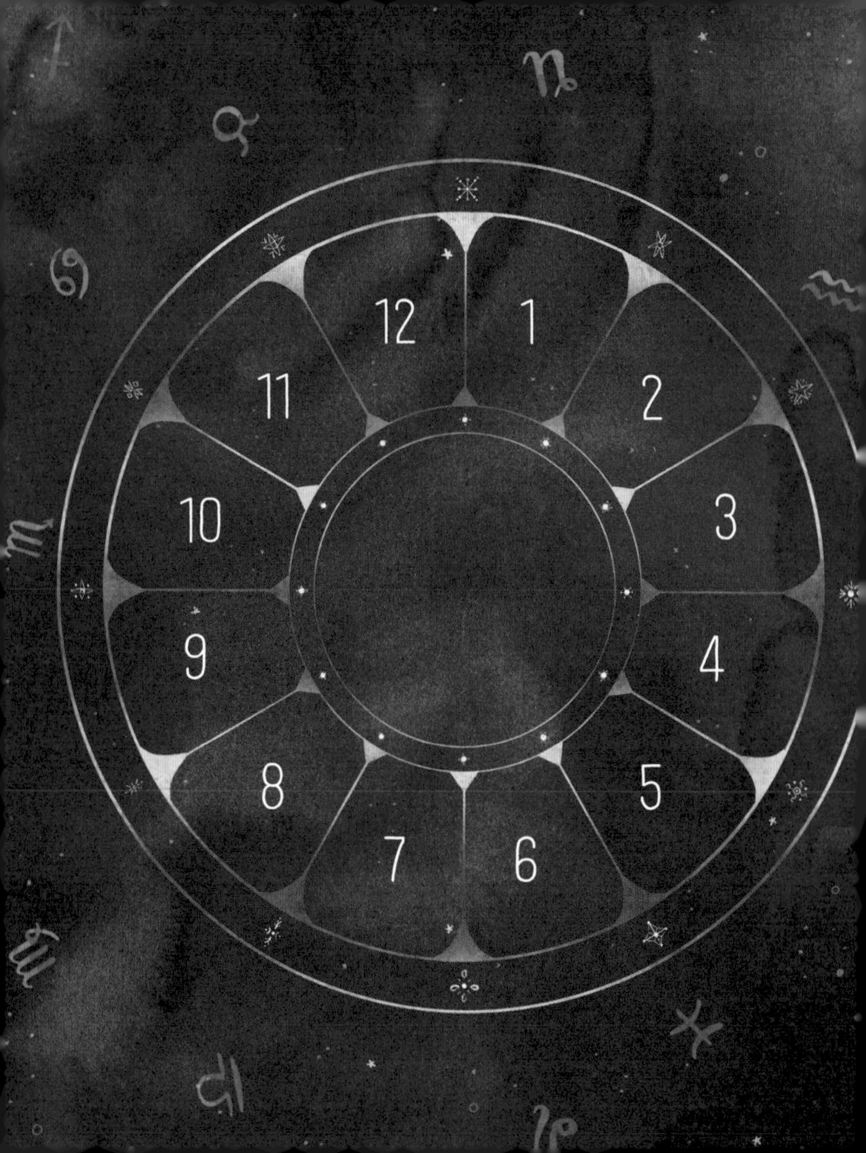

12
1
11
2
10
3
9
4
8
5
7
6

The Twelve Houses

JUST AS THERE ARE TWELVE SIGNS, THERE ARE TWELVE Houses. A "House" is meant to represent an area of life, such as family, work, friendship, etc. Each House contains its own Sign, so that, for instance, your career contains the energy of Aries, or your romantic life contains the energy of Virgo. Again, it's all about information—astrology can provide so much context and insight into how to manage your life.

You can figure out the Signs of your Houses quite easily. Simply place your Ascendant Sign (see page 144) in the first House, and then follow the order of the zodiac as you fill in the other Houses. So, if Libra is your Ascendant Sign, it would also be the Sign of your First House. Then Scorpio would be the Sign of your Second House, Sagittarius of your Third House, and so forth.

FIRST HOUSE • *The House of the Self covers your personality, your body, your appearance, and your self-image.*

SECOND HOUSE • *The House of Worth refers to your self-esteem and what you value, including practical values like money and possessions. The Sign of your Second House will give you insight into how you manage your finances.*

THIRD HOUSE • *The House of Intellect governs your understanding of the world, particularly your immediate surroundings, like your neighborhood and your family.*

FOURTH HOUSE • *The House of the Home includes your literal house, the place where you live, and everything that is a part of that, like your partner, your children, your roommates, and so forth.*

FIFTH HOUSE • *The House of Love covers mostly romantic love, but it may also include friendship, love of family, and more. Like Venus, it also rules creativity, self-expression, and pleasure.*

SIXTH HOUSE • *The House of Work includes your job, of course, but it also refers to the work we do in our daily lives—cooking, cleaning, childcare, diet, fitness, etc.*

SEVENTH HOUSE • *The House of Partnership often refers to marriage, but it may also encompass any relationship where two people must work together.*

EIGHTH HOUSE • *The House of Transformation is about how we exchange money with others, so taxes, investment, mortgages—things like that. It's also about sex and reproduction.*

NINTH HOUSE • *The House of Understanding is a deep and philosophical place. It governs dreams, visions, ideas, ethics, and rituals.*

TENTH HOUSE • *The House of Status helps us understand how others see us and where we excel.*

ELEVENTH HOUSE • *The House of Friendship is about community, how we come together with the people in our lives.*

TWELFTH HOUSE • *The House of the Subconscious governs the self that we cannot always see or recognize. It includes our dreams, our intuition, and our secrets.*

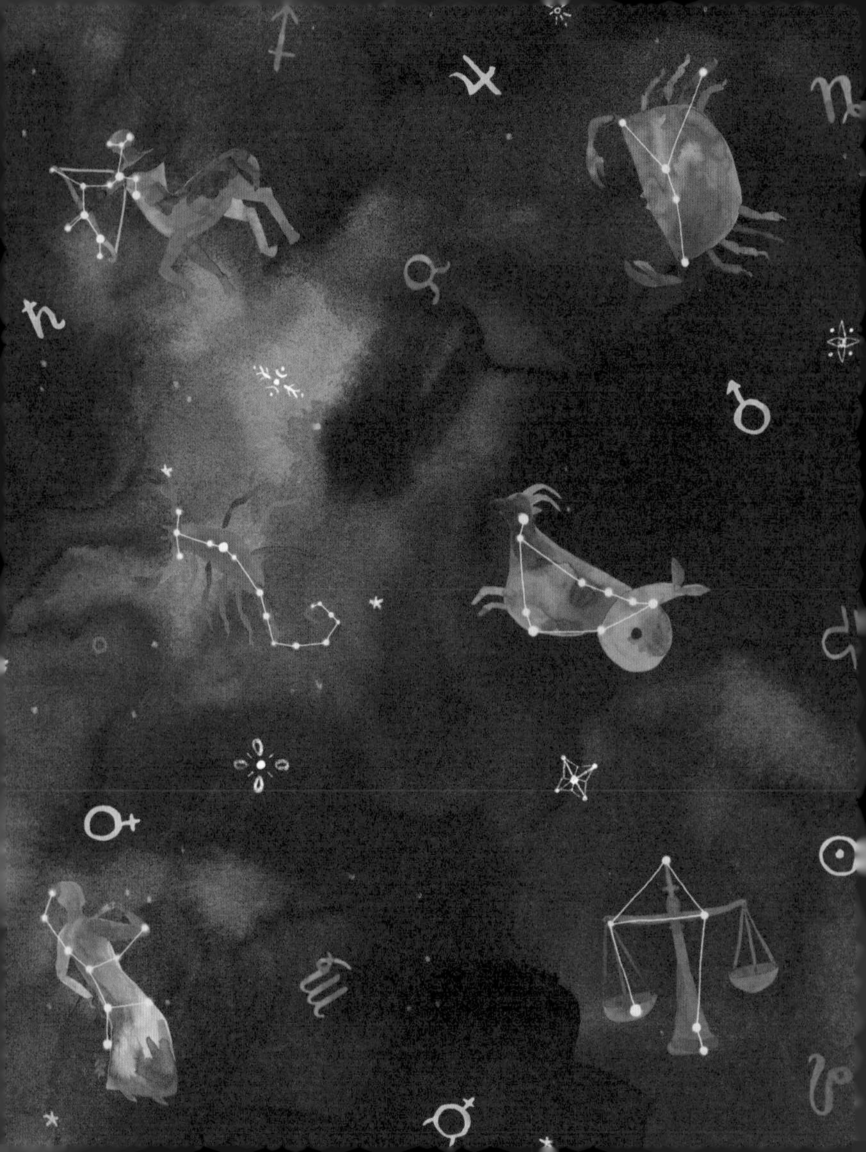

The Signs

ARIES

You are a born leader. You are brave, competitive, energetic, quick-thinking, and confident. You are a trailblazer, and you push those around you to move outside their self-assigned boxes. You never back down from a fight . . . and so sometimes you can be a little impulsive and aggressive.

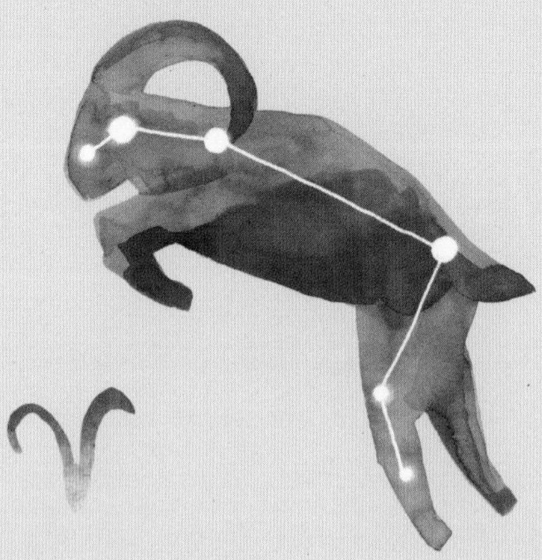

BIRTH DATE:	RULER:	BEST PAIRED WITH:
March 21–April 19	Mars	Other Aries, Gemini, Leo, and Libra

TAURUS

You are practical and hardworking, like all Earth Signs, but you are also sensual and have a deep appreciation for beauty. You are always prepared, and you can think ahead, anticipating troubles that might come up. Yes, you are stubborn, but that stubbornness can make you incredibly loyal. You can be a little overprotective and sometimes have trouble compromising. You are more sensitive than people realize and can get your feelings hurt.

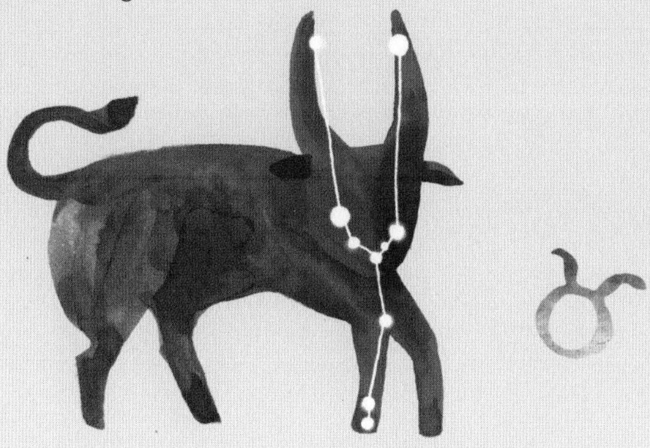

BIRTH DATE:	RULER:	BEST PAIRED WITH:
April 20–May 20	Venus	Virgo, Capricorn, and Cancer

GEMINI

You've got a lot going on! Your moodiness is a part of you—sometimes you are fun and playful, and other times you can be quiet and introspective. You sometimes have trouble making decisions, but you are great at communication. You take so much joy in the world and share that joy with others.

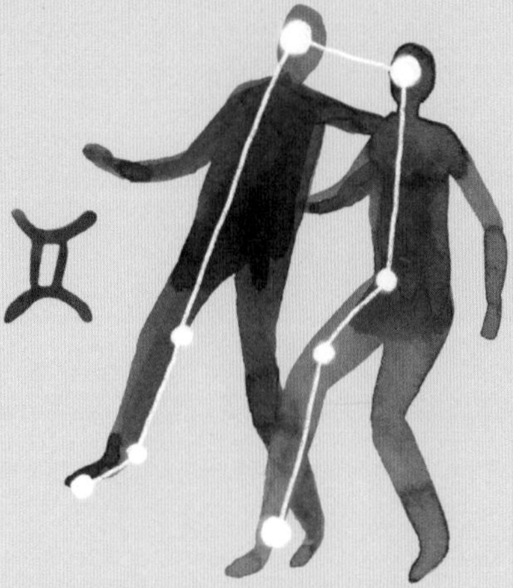

BIRTH DATE:	RULER:	BEST PAIRED WITH:
May 21–June 20	Mercury	Leo, Libra, Aquarius, and Aries

CANCER

You care deeply about those close to you. You are empathetic and emotional, which can sometimes make you a bit moody and insecure, bringing out your protective side. You thrive on harmony—when others are happy, you're happy. Your kindness and thoughtfulness can sometimes lead you to sacrifice your happiness for the sake of others.

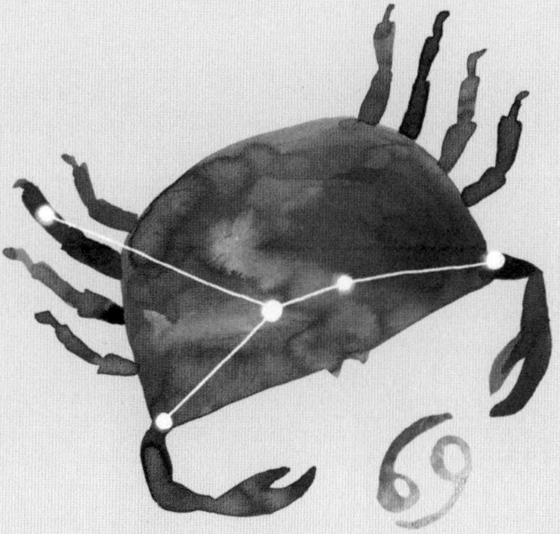

BIRTH DATE:	RULER:	BEST PAIRED WITH:
June 21–July 22	Moon	Other Cancers, Scorpio, Virgo, Pisces, and Taurus

LEO

You are creative and passionate—you love life and you love solving problems. You can seem like a drama queen, because you do love attention, but really you just want to be seen for who you really are. You have a great sense of humor, and your energy brings others to you, like planets orbiting the sun.

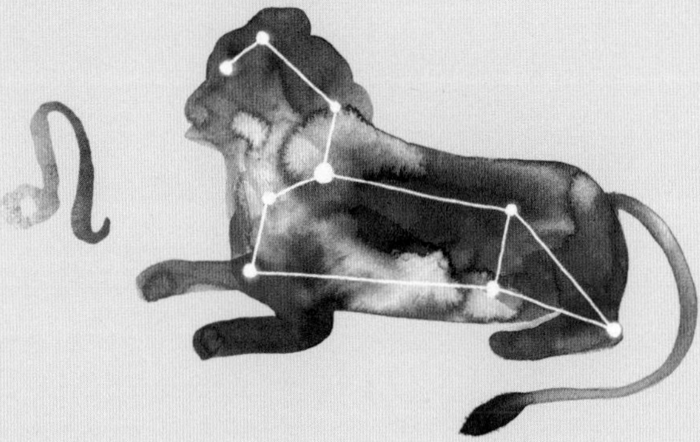

BIRTH DATE:	RULER:	BEST PAIRED WITH:
July 23–August 22	Sun	Other Leos, Aries, Gemini, Libra, and Sagittarius

VIRGO

You are very organized, polite, and self-aware, but you are also deeply empathetic and insightful. You can be a little shy, and you can be critical, both of others and of yourself. Your shyness sometimes masks how deeply you care for others.

BIRTH DATE:	RULER:	BEST PAIRED WITH:
August 23–September 22	Mercury	Taurus, Cancer, Capricorn, and Scorpio

LIBRA

You are peaceful and fair, and value partnership and cooperation. You are highly intelligent, and love to surround yourself with smart, engaged, creative people. You don't like conflict, but when it does arise, you are a good mediator—though sometimes you neglect your own grudges.

BIRTH DATE:	RULER:	BEST PAIRED WITH:
September 23–October 22	Venus	Gemini, Leo, Sagittarius, and Aquarius

SCORPIO

You can be a little mysterious, but it's because you are an intensely private person. That said, you do feel things deeply and have no trouble expressing your emotions when talking with someone you trust. You are driven and decisive, and value authenticity and truth in others.

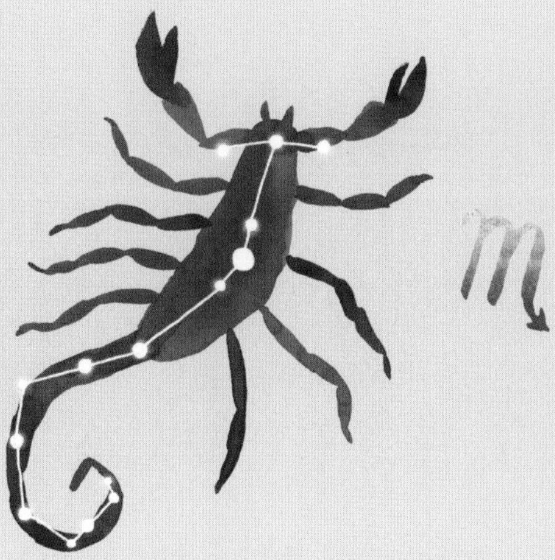

BIRTH DATE:	RULER:	BEST PAIRED WITH:
October 23–November 21	Mars	Cancer, Pisces, Taurus, Capricorn, and Virgo

SAGITTARIUS

You find so much joy in life. You are intensely curious and want to know and experience everything the world has to offer. You're funny and imaginative, but you also think deeply about things. You're not so great at following rules, mostly because you are impatient.

BIRTH DATE:	RULER:	BEST PAIRED WITH:
November 22–December 21	Jupiter	Aries, Libra, Aquarius, and Leo

CAPRICORN

You can seem a little serious, but that's because you are responsible, practical, and tend to focus on what's most important to you. You are ambitious, and so you work hard, and you are also loyal and put effort into making your friends and loved ones feel how much they matter to you.

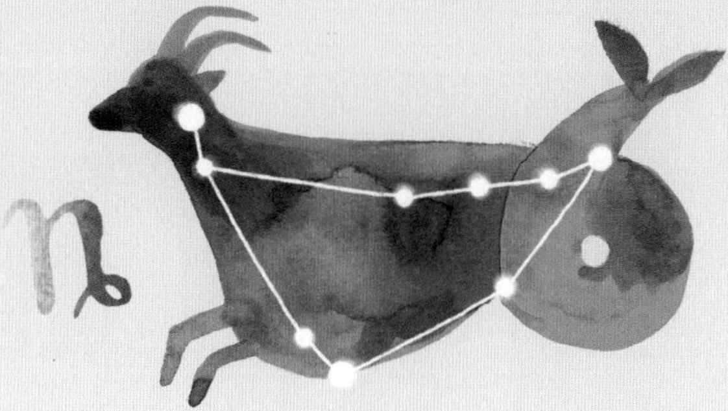

BIRTH DATE:	RULER:	BEST PAIRED WITH:
December 22–January 19	Saturn	Other Capricorns, Taurus, Virgo, and Pisces

AQUARIUS

You can sometimes come off as reserved, but you're really just deep in thought. You do like to know people well before you let them get to know the real you, but once they do, you are a great friend. You love to help, though you do require some alone time. You are always working to evolve, to become the best version of yourself.

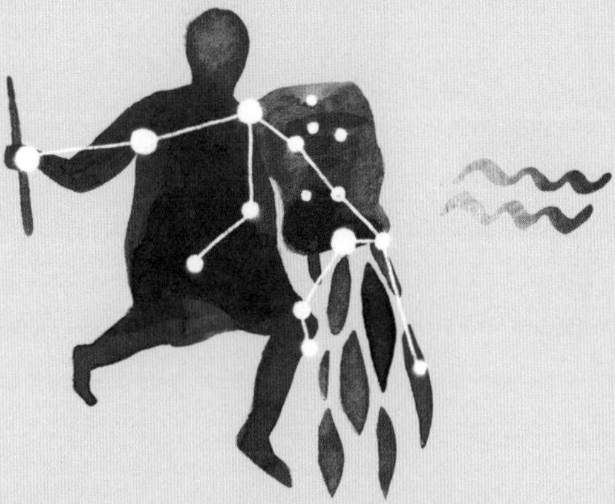

BIRTH DATE:	RULER:	BEST PAIRED WITH:
January 20—February 18	Uranus	Gemini, Sagittarius, Aries, and Libra

PISCES

You are friendly and artistic, intuitive and empathetic. You are also imaginative and dreamy. You have lots of friends, and they are drawn to you because your internal wisdom gives you insight and also makes you gentle and tolerant. You tend to have deep and lasting relationships.

BIRTH DATE:	RULER:	BEST PAIRED WITH:
February 19–March 20	Neptune	Scorpio, Cancer, Taurus, and Capricorn

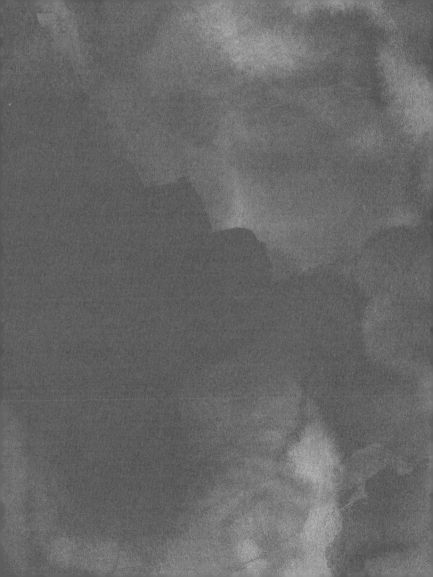

REFERENCES

Einstein, Albert. *The Principle of Relativity*. "Does the Inertia of a Body Depend upon Its Energy-Content." Translated by W. Perrett and G.B. Jeffery. London: Methuen and Company, 1923.

Hall, Judy. *101 Power Crystals: The Ultimate Guide to Magical Crystals, Gems, and Stones for Healing and Transformation*. Beverly, MA: Fair Winds Press, 2011.

Khalsa, Dharma Singh, and Cameron Stauth. *Meditation as Medicine: Activate the Power of Your Natural Healing Force*. New York: Simon & Schuster, 2009.

Randall, David K. *Dreamland: Adventures in the Strange Science of Sleep*. New York: W.W. Norton & Company, 2012.

Raphael, Katrina. *Crystal Enlightenment, Vol. 1: The Transforming Properties of Crystals and Healing Stones.* Santa Fe, NM: Aurora Press, 1985.

Simmons, Robert. *The Pocket Book of Stones: Who They Are & What They Teach*. Berkeley, CA: North Atlantic Book, 2015.

St. Clair, Kassia. *The Secret Lives of Color*. New York: Penguin Books, 2016.

Tzu, Lao. *Tao Te Ching: A Book About the Way and the Power of the Way*. Translated by Ursula K. Le Guin. Boulder, CO: Shambhala Publications, 1998.

Watts, Alan. *The Wisdom of Insecurity: A Message for an Age of Anxiety*. Second Vintage Edition. New York: Vintage Books, 2011.

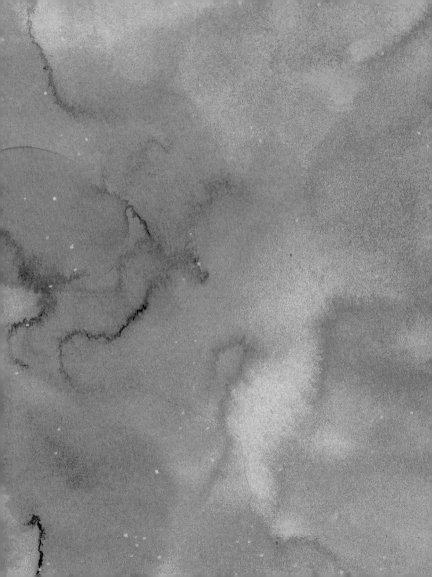